A Note From Rick Renner

I am on a personal quest to see a "revival of the Bible" so people can establish their lives on a firm foundation that will stand strong and endure the test as end-time storm winds begin to intensify.

In order to experience a revival of the Bible in your personal life, it is important to take time each day to read, receive, and apply its truths to your life. James tells us that if we will continue in the perfect law of liberty — refusing to be forgetful hearers, but determined to be doers — we will be blessed in our ways. As you watch or listen to the programs in this series and work through this corresponding study guide, I trust you will search the Scriptures and allow the Holy Spirit to help you hear something new from God's Word that applies specifically to your life. I encourage you to be a doer of the Word He reveals to you. Whatever the cost, I assure you — it will be worth it.

> Thy words were found, and I did eat them;
> and thy word was unto me the joy and rejoicing of mine heart:
> for I am called by thy name, O Lord God of hosts.
> — Jeremiah 15:16

Your brother and friend in Jesus Christ,

Rick Renner

'Prejudiced — Me?'
Overcoming Prejudice in the Church and in Your Life

Copyright © 2025 by Rick Renner
1814 W. Tacoma St.
Broken Arrow, OK 74012-1406

Published by Rick Renner Ministries
www.renner.org

ISBN 13: 978-1-6675-1219-8

ISBN 13 eBook: 978-1-6675-1220-4

How To Use This Study Guide

This five-lesson study guide corresponds to *"Prejudiced — Me? Overcoming Prejudice in the Church and in Your Life" With Rick Renner* (Renner TV). Each lesson in this study guide covers a topic that is addressed during the program series, with questions and references supplied to draw you deeper into your own private study of the Scriptures on this subject.

To derive the most benefit from this study guide, consider the following:

First, watch or listen to the program prior to working through the corresponding lesson in this guide. (Programs can also be viewed at **renner.org** by clicking on the Media/Archives links or on our Renner Ministries YouTube channel.)

Second, take the time to look up the scriptures included in each lesson. Prayerfully consider their application to your own life.

Third, use a journal or notebook to make note of your answers to each lesson's Study Questions and Practical Application challenges.

Fourth, invest specific time in prayer and in the Word of God to consult with the Holy Spirit. Write down the scriptures or insights He reveals to you.

Finally, take action! Whatever the Lord tells you to do according to His Word, do it.

For added insights on this subject, it is recommended that you obtain Rick Renner's books *Sparkling Gems from the Greek, Volumes 1 and 2*. You may also select from Rick's other available resources by placing your order at **renner.org** or by calling 1-800-742-5593.

TOPIC

So You Think You're Not Prejudiced?

SCRIPTURES

1. **James 2:1** — My brethren, have not the faith of our Lord Jesus Christ, the Lord of glory, with respect of persons.

2. **1 Samuel 16:7** — ...For the Lord seeth not as man seeth; for man looketh on the outward appearance, but the Lord looketh on the heart.

GREEK WORDS

1. "respect of persons" — **προσωποληψία** (*prosopolepsia*): a compound of **πρόσωπον** (*prosopon*), which means peering directly into the face of another, and **λαμβάνω** (*lambano*), which most often means to receive or to take; compounded, it literally means looking at one's face or looking at one's external appearance

SYNOPSIS

The five lessons in this study titled *'Prejudiced — Me?' Overcoming Prejudice in the Church and in Your Life* will focus on the following topics:

- So You Think You're Not Prejudiced?
- Distinctions Should Disappear in Jesus Christ
- We Are All One in Jesus Christ
- Ethnic and Class Differences Do Not Exist in Christ
- Five Things To Do If You Have Prejudice

Prejudice is a real problem — both in society and even in the Church. The variety of prejudices is seemingly endless, and while we appear to be able to quickly identify prejudice in others, it is often very difficult to see it in ourselves. In this lesson, we will examine dozens of forms of prejudice, some of which you may have never heard. Open your heart and allow the Holy Spirit to shine His searchlight, exposing any prejudice you may not be aware of in your life.

The emphasis of this lesson:

The Bible clearly commands us as believers in Christ to not have prejudice toward others. Essentially, to be prejudiced is to pre-judge. It is an unfavorable, preconceived opinion that is formed against a person or group without just grounds. Although prejudice comes in countless forms, it is not natural or normal.

James Candidly Commanded Believers Not To Be Prejudiced

James, the half-brother of Jesus, wrote a letter to many First Century believers who had been scattered across the Roman Empire due to government persecution. These early believers faced not only the challenge of living as exiles in foreign lands but also the pressure of navigating a society deeply divided by class, status, and ethnicity. In the second chapter of this letter, James gave a strong admonition:

> **My brethren, have not the faith of our Lord Jesus Christ, the Lord of glory, with respect of persons.**
>
> **—James 2:1**

If we make an honest evaluation of this passage, there is no question that James was instructing us — under the unction of the Holy Spirit — to not be prejudiced against others. But what exactly is prejudice? And how does it manifest in our daily lives?

The Basic Meaning of 'Prejudice'

The basic meaning of the word "prejudice" is to *pre-judge*. It refers to forming an opinion or an unreasonable dislike toward a person or group without having a personal experience with them. To be prejudiced is to have an irrational attitude of dislike or even hostility directed against an individual, a group, a race, or their supposed characteristics. It is an adverse opinion or formed without just grounds — a preconceived judgment or preconceived opinion.

Prejudices can strongly influence how people behave and interact with others. While it is often subconscious, it can affect people's behavior without their realizing it. Some features of prejudice include negative feelings and stereotypical beliefs about members of a group. When individuals hold prejudicial attitudes toward others, they tend to view everyone in a particular group as the same, and if that prejudice is not corrected, it can lead to discrimination.

Since we've laid a foundation for the meaning of the word "prejudice," let's return to James 2:1, which says, "My brethren, have not the faith of our Lord Jesus Christ, the Lord of glory, with respect of persons."

Factoring in the original Greek meaning of this passage, the *Renner Interpretive Version (RIV)* of James 2:1 says:

> **My dearest brothers and comrades, whom I cherish and treasure, you must not be a respecter of persons. That is, you must not have, hold, and possess the faith of our Lord Jesus Christ, the Lord of glory — and at the same time judge others or base your acceptance of them by what you see in their external appearance.**

An interesting footnote to this verse in the *Renner Interpretive Version (RIV)* is Footnote 232, which provides further insight into the phrase "respect of persons." The Greek word used here is *prosopolepsia*, which literally means *looking at one's face* or *looking at one's external appearance*. The Greek word *prosopolepsia* consists of the blending together of the word *prosopon*, which means *peering directly into the face of another*, and *lambano*, which most often means *to receive or to take*. When you compound these two words to form the word *prosopolepsia*, it means *to take your opinion or judgment about somebody according to his or her face or external appearance.*[1]

The Bible states that this is evil. Judging others by outward appearance is wrong. This was made quite clear in First Samuel 16:7, where God declared:

> **...For the Lord seeth not as man seeth; for man looketh on the outward appearance, but the Lord looketh on the heart.**

If God looks at a person's heart rather than at his or her outward appearance, then we, as believers, should strive to do the same.

To be clear, being *prejudiced* is not the same as having a *preference*. Having preferences — for example, choosing certain foods over others — is not inherently wrong. However, prejudice involves making pre-judgments about others before knowing who they truly are and what is in their hearts. This is not what God calls us to do.

Prejudice Against Blacks
Was Rampant in Rick's Younger Days

One of the most common ways prejudice forms is through judging others by their appearance — especially by the color of their skin. As a rule, people seem to be particularly prejudiced against anyone with darker skin color. Several decades ago, there was a particularly egregious prevalence of *black prejudice* in our country. In fact, it was so strong that there was a time in our country when there were separate schools for whites and blacks. Likewise, there were also separate restaurants and separate churches.

But the segregation didn't stop there. History documents that there were also separate drinking fountains and separate toilets for whites and blacks. Moreover, there was separate seating in movie theaters, separate seating on public transportation, and separate neighborhoods for those who were white and those who were black. There were even despicable ordinances in some towns stating that blacks could not walk on the sidewalk with whites.

Even more shocking were areas known as "sundown towns" in which black people were not allowed to be out of their homes after sundown. Denise Renner, who grew up without a prejudiced bone in her body toward black people, lived in such a town as a child in northeastern Oklahoma.

Years later, Denise trained operatically under a fabulously talented and famous couple who were black opera singers. Tragically, the man's wife, who was one of the premier opera singers at the time, was not allowed to perform on stage in New York City because of the color of her skin. Although it is grieving to cite these absolutely terrible and unthinkable facts, thank God a great deal of this form of prejudice is being broken off the minds of many. But that is not enough. As believers, we must continue to pray that this mindset be completely eradicated, never to return.

Many Forms of Prejudice Exist

Of course, prejudice against black people isn't the only form of prejudice — there are countless others. For example, there are individuals who are prejudiced toward white people, Asians, and Native Americans. There is also a prejudice against Jewish people, which is often referred to as antisemitism.

Likewise, there is German prejudice, which was particularly strong after World War II. Rick shared how one of his own relatives, whose last name was Renner, changed his name to another, slightly different form of Renner so that people would think he was French. He didn't want anyone to know that he was a German, because there was such prejudice against Germans at that time.

It is probably safe to say that wherever there are differences between human beings, prejudice is often lurking beneath the surface just waiting to come forth. It may manifest in subtle ways, such as through stereotypes or behaviors toward others, or in more overt and harmful actions. Regardless of how it appears, prejudice creates unnecessary division, and it is our responsibility to recognize and resist it whenever it arises.

Prejudice Goes Beyond the Color of One's Skin

Not all prejudice is based on appearance. Rick shared how when he, Denise, and their family moved to Riga, Latvia more than three decades ago, all the people there were light-skinned. Yet, there was a staunch prejudice between those who were Latvians and those who were Russian. Although the people looked and sounded the same, they were prejudiced against each other because of past conflicts that left a bitterness between them.

The same is true in Europe. In that region, most people are generally white- or light-skinned, but that doesn't change the fact that there is prejudice that exists between the British and the French, the French and the Germans, the Germans and the Italians, and the Italians and the Polish. Even though the populace all basically look the same, there is strong prejudice between these different people groups, and the same can be said about people within the Asian communities.

At the Moscow Good News Church, there are many Africans who attend. But even though they are all from the continent of Africa, they are from different nations. Consequently, they have a lot of strong feelings toward each other. Thus, prejudice is not all about skin color and nationality. Sometimes it arises from historical or cultural factors that go far beyond mere appearance.

A List of Common and Not-So-Common Prejudices

In addition to skin color prejudice — whether against black, brown, white, or other tones — there is also **age prejudice**. For instance, prejudiced young people could deem the older generations as useless and a liability that requires a burdensome amount of care and attention.

In contrast, some older people could harbor prejudice against the young, labeling them as inexperienced, selfish, and overly reliant on technology. Some older individuals may see younger people as lacking work ethic or direction, assuming that they have no money or lack responsibility, while some of the younger individuals perceive their elders as overbearing, needy, and outdated. In this way, both the young and the old can develop prejudices against each other.

There is also **class prejudice** between the rich and the poor. Some poor people view anyone who is rich as being wicked and evil, while some rich people view the poor as wretched and useless to society. Surprisingly, there are even poor people who find reason to be prejudiced against other poor people.

How about **unmarried prejudice**? This is when married people look at others who've reached a certain age and are not married and think that something is wrong with them. This is yet another form of prejudice.

Then there's **educated and uneducated prejudice**. An example of this is when some educated people consider themselves to be better than others who have not been formally educated. But it goes both ways. There are some people who lack a formal education and look down on those who are educated, calling them snooty or pretentious.

Sadly, **disabilities prejudice** also exists. This is when someone has the wrong opinion about those who have physical, developmental, or learning disabilities that limit what they can do. There's also **physical-anomaly prejudice** toward people with physical abnormalities like acne, deformities, extra fingers, or complications with the eyes or ears.

Oddly enough, there is also **voice prejudice**. This is when individuals treat people differently according to their voice tones. Specifically, some people dislike and are irritated by those with high-pitched voices, preferring those with lower voices that seem to be easier on the ears.

Orphan prejudice is another type of discrimination in which some people have a negative attitude toward orphans, believing them to be thieves that can't be trusted or looking down on them. Then there is **homeless-person prejudice**. This is when some people take on the erroneous mindset that all homeless people are drunks or drug addicts who don't take life seriously. The truth is, many homeless people are highly educated individuals who at one time were tremendously successful before hitting hard times in life.

Gender prejudice also exists where people have a bad attitude toward someone simply because that person is male or female. Some individuals even have **female-boss prejudice,** which is when someone is biased against women being the top manager or in a position of authority. The belief that men are superior to women is often referred to as **male chauvinism**.

Other preconceived judgmental attitudes include people who believe all first-born children are overachievers who did everything correctly right from the start; middle children are neutral negotiators; and the youngest child has it the easiest and is always spoiled.

How about **hair-color prejudice**? Some people automatically believe that all blonds are ditzy, and all redheads are hotheads. The list continues with **tattoo prejudice,** in which some people automatically form a negative judgment about someone with a tattoo, and **bodybuilders prejudice,** which is the wrong belief that those who are full of muscles lack intelligence. There is also **beard prejudice**. Shockingly, this is when some people are okay with certain lengths or types of beards, but they're not okay with others.

Families-with-no-children prejudice is also real. Some people will look at a couple who has no children and think, *Those people are just selfish and living for themselves.* At the same time, there is also **families-with-a-lot-of-children prejudice**. In this case, some individuals pre-judge families with many children, calling the parents uneducated and irresponsible for continuing to have child after child. Both preconceived judgments are wrong.

How about **mother-in-law prejudice, prisoner prejudice, debt prejudice,** or **name prejudice**? Strangely, there are some people who don't trust or like others with a particular name due to an experience with someone else with the same name. Then there's **medication prejudice** in which people form harsh, negative opinions of others because they take a lot of medication. Similarly, some people have **former-drug-addict prejudice,** believing the false notion, "once a drug addict, always a drug addict," which is simply not true. Although many people who struggle with drug addiction revert to their old ways after rehabilitation efforts, many people — especially after coming to know Jesus — overcome their addiction.

Another form of pre-judging is **weight prejudice**. When some people notice that a person is overweight, they automatically assume that person is undisciplined or lazy. On the other hand, there is also **skinny-people prejudice** in which thin individuals are viewed as weak, sickly, or troubled. This demonstrates how when prejudice enters the picture, you just can't win.

What about **foreigner** or **immigrant prejudice**? This is when someone treats others poorly simply because they are from a different country or culture than his own. Another one is **city prejudice** — when someone forms a judgment about others who live in a particular city. Jesus, Himself, dealt with this one. When He was introduced as being from Nazareth, a certain person replied, "…Can anything good come out of Nazareth?" (John 1:46).

The list continues with **language prejudice** and **accent prejudice** in which people form negative opinions about those who speak certain languages or have accents they don't like. Then there is **North/South prejudice**, which is when some southerners are prejudiced against northerners, claiming northerners are hard-nosed and uncaring, and some northerners are prejudiced against southerners, believing them to be slow and unintelligent.

Then there are numerous related types of prejudice such as **musical** and **artistic prejudice**, which is when an artist or musician forms a negative opinion of other artists who aren't of the same genre or style. There is also **clothing prejudice** in which people make judgments about others based on what they wear.

Even in the Church we find things like **worship-style prejudice**; **denominational prejudice**; **large-church** and **small-church prejudice**; **Bible-translation prejudice**; **pastors-of-small-churches prejudice**; and **pastors-of-large-churches prejudice**. And, of course, **religious prejudice** is a major issue causing many Muslims to hate Jews, many Jews to hate Muslims, and on and on it goes.

Prejudice Isn't Normal or Natural

To be clear — prejudice is not natural, and no one is born with it. Prejudice is acquired from an outside source. It is often transferred to you through negative life experiences, leading you to unfairly judge a certain group of people based on how you were treated.

Prejudice can also be passed on to you by culture and society, by education, by family, or by friends. It's taught by people who transfer their bad experiences to you or to someone else. While there may be "reasons" for all forms of prejudice, in the Church, there are no excuses for it. Regardless of where we picked it up, all prejudice is ungodly, wicked, and has no place among the people of God.

In our next lesson, we will carefully unpack James 2:1-4 and see that, as Christians, all distinctions disappear in Jesus Christ.

STUDY QUESTIONS

Study to shew thyself approved unto God, a workman that needeth not to be ashamed, rightly dividing the word of truth.
— 2 Timothy 2:15

1. James 2:1 tells us we are not to be a "respecter of persons." How does this coincide with Job 34:18 and 19; Acts 10:34 and 35; Romans 2:1 and 10:11-13; and Ephesians 6:9? What characteristic of God is repeatedly identified in these verses? How grateful are you that He feels this way toward you?

2. The prophet Isaiah gave us a clear picture of how Jesus Himself judged people when He walked on the earth. Consider Isaiah 11:1-4 and identify how Jesus assessed and evaluated people. According to verses 2 and 3, what empowered Him to act in this way (also *see* John 3:34)? Pray and ask God to empower you in this same way (*see* John 1:16; Ephesians 5:18; and Colossians 2:9,10.)

PRACTICAL APPLICATION

But be ye doers of the word, and not hearers only, deceiving your own selves.
—James 1:22

1. Prejudices can strongly influence how we behave and interact with others. They are often operating subconsciously and can affect our behavior without us even realizing it. As you read through the list of more than 40 different types of prejudice, what did you sense in your heart? Be honest, did you identify with any of the pre-judging scenarios presented? If so, which one(s) stood out to you? What negative feelings and stereotypical beliefs are you dealing with?

2. Take time now to be honest with God and bring any wrong attitudes and actions to Him in prayer. He wants to heal your hurts and set you free from all forms of prejudice, if you'll let Him.

NOTES

[1]Rick Renner. *Renner Interpretive Version — James and Jude* (Shippensburg, PA: Harrison House Publishers, 2024), pg. 60.

TOPIC

Distinctions Should Disappear in Jesus Christ

SCRIPTURES

1. **James 2:1** — My brethren, have not the faith of our Lord Jesus Christ, the Lord of glory, with respect of persons.
2. **1 Samuel 16:7** — ...For the Lord seeth not as man seeth; for man looketh on the outward appearance, but the Lord looketh on the heart.
3. **James 2:2** — For if there come unto your assembly a man with a gold ring, in goodly apparel, and there come in also a poor man in vile raiment.
4. **James 2:3** — And ye have respect to him that weareth the gay clothing, and say unto him, Sit thou here in a good place; and say to the poor, Stand thou there, or sit here under my footstool.
5. **James 2:4** — Are ye not then partial in yourselves, and are become judges of evil thoughts?
6. **2 Corinthians 5:16** — Wherefore henceforth know we no man after the flesh....
7. **2 Corinthians 5:17** — Therefore if any man be in Christ, he is a new creature: old things are passed away; behold, all things are become new.

GREEK WORDS

1. "respect of persons" — **προσωποληψία** (*prosopolepsia*): a compound of **πρόσωπον** (*prosopon*), which means peering directly into the face of another, and **λαμβάνω** (*lambano*), which most often means to receive or to take; compounded, it literally means looking at one's face or looking at one's external appearance

2. "if"— **εἰ** (*ei*)" a condition particle, which assumes that what follows is or probably will be the case

3. "a gold ring" — **χρυσοδακτύλιος** (*chrusodaktulios*): a compound of **χρυσός** (*chrusos*), which pictures the highest grade and the most expensive form of gold, and **δακτύλιος** (*daktulios*), which refers to a fabulous ring that is highly decorated; as a compound, it pictures a highly decorated golden ring of great value

4. "in goodly apparel" — **ἐσθῆτι λαμπρᾷ** (*estheti lampra*): a compound of the word **ἐσθής** (*esthes*), which pictures a robe or vestment, and the word **λαμπρός** (*lampros*), which means bright, gorgeous, magnificent, resplendent, shining, or sumptuous; compounded, it refers to clothing that is obviously expensive and belongs to someone with financial means

5. "then" — **δὲ** (*de*): a conjunction intended to make a dramatic comparison

6. "poor man" — **πτωχὸς** (*ptochos*): one who crouches or cowers like a beggar — probably out of embarrassment for the way he looks; it describes abject poverty; one who is beggarly, deeply destitute, lacking in earthly resources, or poor; one who is a pauper; a person so destitute that he is deprived of the barest essentials for living; a homeless person; someone who has to scrounge to find enough food to eat; a person society would consider down and out, financially ruined, and poverty-stricken; a social outcast

7. "vile" — **ῥυπαρός** (*rhuparos*): it depicts that which is filthy, dirty, grimy, or rank

8. "vile raiment" — **ῥυπαρᾷ ἐσθῆτι** (*rhupara estheti*): it portrays filthy, dirty, grimy, rank clothes or one who dresses as if he lives in squalor; it carries the idea of a person dressed in dirty, grimy, and offensively stinking clothes

9. "partial" — **διακρίνω** (*diakrino*): a compound of the preposition **διά** (*dia*) and the word **κρίνω** (*krino*). The word **διά** (*dia*) means through and depicts something that is done very thoroughly. The word **κρίνω**

(*krino*) pictures a verdict or final sentence pronounced as the result of a court trial. Compounded, it pictures one who has wrangled back and forth with the evidence he has seen with his eyes, and — after weighing all the evidence — he comes to a conclusion and passes a final judgment

10. "evil thoughts" — πονηρός (*poneros*): to be malicious or malignant; it pictures whatever is foul, hostile, vicious, and vile; it includes not only that which is dangerous to the physical body, but also that which is dangerous to the spirit or mind; it is an act or attitude that is wicked, unholy, and impure in the sight of God

SYNOPSIS

In the Early Church, especially in Jerusalem, prejudice existed, but it wasn't based on skin color or nationality. The prejudice that prevailed in the Church was between the rich and the poor. Evidently, those with money and affluence were celebrated and given preferential treatment, whereas the poor were tolerated and treated as second-class citizens. James was aware of this evil double standard that was taking place, and he called on believers to put it out of their lives.

The emphasis of this lesson:

The Bible says both rich and poor will make their way into the Church, and although it's hard not to be drawn in by the flashiness of the wealthy, we must guard against treating them more favorably than the poor. This type of prejudice and discrimination is evil in God's eyes.

A Brief Review of James 2:1

As we learned in Lesson 1, James, the half-brother of Jesus, wrote to persecuted believers that had been dispersed throughout the Roman empire during the First Century, encouraging them to stay strong in Christ, despite the opposition coming against them. At the same time, he brought correction to them, including these words of instruction in James 2:1:

> **My brethren, have not the faith of our Lord Jesus Christ, the Lord of glory, with respect of persons.**

When we factor in the original Greek meaning of the key words in this verse, the *Renner Interpretive Version* (*RIV*) of James 2:1 says:

My dearest brothers and comrades, whom I cherish and treasure, you must not be a respecter of persons. That is, you must not have, hold, and possess the faith of our Lord Jesus Christ, the Lord of glory — and at the same time judge others or base your acceptance of them by what you see in their external appearance.

In the *Renner Interpretive Version* (*RIV*), Footnote 232 provides interesting insight into the phrase "respect of persons." In the Greek, this phrase is translated from *prosopolepsia*, which literally means *looking at one's face or looking at one's external appearance*…. The Greek word *prosopolepsia* consists of the blending together of the word *prosopon*, which means *peering directly into the face of another*, and *lambano*, which most often means *to receive* or *to take*. When compounded, these words form the word *prosopolepsia*, meaning *to take your opinion or your judgment about somebody according to his face or according to his external appearance*.[1] And as we noted in Lesson 1, the Bible warns against this, telling us clearly:

> **…For the Lord seeth not as man seeth; for man looketh on the outward appearance, but the Lord looketh on the heart.**
> **— 1 Samuel 16:7**

In a world that chooses to judge others by appearances rather than "looking on the heart," it is essential for believers to internalize this truth: God calls us to seek the inherent worth in every person, regardless of societal status or outward appearance. It's God's will that we reflect God's love and grace to all, regardless of his or her differences in appearance or circumstance.

Both Rich and Poor Were Coming Into the Church

James' teaching in James 2:1 was especially relevant to the Early Church, where believers from all walks of life — both the wealthy and the poor — were coming together as one body. However, this unity was not without its challenges. Favoritism crept into their gatherings, creating tensions that needed to be addressed. What was going on among the believers to which James was writing? We begin to get a snapshot of what was taking place in James 2:2, where James said:

For if there come unto your assembly a man with a gold ring, in goodly apparel, and there come in also a poor man in vile raiment.

Here we see that there was quite a social and economic disparity among those who were coming into the church of Jerusalem. There were very wealthy people and also those who were extremely poor. Yet despite these disparities, they were all gathering in the same place.

When we factor in the original Greek meaning of the key words in the very beginning of this verse, the *Renner Interpretive Version* (*RIV*) of the first part of James 2:2 says:

For if — as it will surely happen from time to time....

Footnote 233 in the *Renner Interpretive Version* (*RIV*), says, "The words 'if — as it will happen from time to time' are a translation of a form of *ei*, a conditional particle, which assumes that what follows is or probably will be the case."[2] Thus, from time to time, both the rich and the poor were coming into church.

It's Hard Not To Notice the Flashiness of the Rich

This interpretation of James 2:2 reinforces the idea that the presence of both rich and poor believers in the congregation was not merely hypothetical but a reality in the Early Church. The diversity of wealth and status among believers was something they regularly encountered, making James' message especially relevant to their typical interactions.

The *Renner Interpretive Version* (*RIV*) of James 2:2 goes on to say:

...There comes a man into your congregation with a fabulously designed, expensive gold ring....

To understand the additional text here, we turn to Footnote 235 in the *Renner Interpretive Version* (*RIV*), which says, "The words 'a fabulously designed, expensive gold ring' are an interpretation of the word *chrusodaktulios*, which is derived from the words *chrusos* and *daktulios*. The word *chrusos* pictures *the highest grade and the most expensive form of gold*, and the word *daktulios* refers to *a fabulous ring that is highly decorated*. As a compound, it pictures *a highly decorated golden ring of great value*."[3]

So according to James 2:2, from time to time, a man came walking into the congregation, and the people noticed his very expensive ring, which is not out of the ordinary. If you were in a similar situation, you would probably notice it too, as you would've most likely noticed when a woman came in with dazzling diamonds around her wrist or neck.

The *Renner Interpretive Version* (*RIV*) of James 2:2 continues to say:

> **…There comes a man into your congregation with a fabulously designed, expensive gold ring and is dressed in obviously expensive, plush, sumptuous clothes….**

Footnote 236 in the *Renner Interpretive Version* (*RIV*) tells us, "The words 'obviously expensive, plush, sumptuous clothes' are an interpretation of the words *estheti lampra*…. The word *esthes*…pictures *a robe or vestment*, and the word *lampros*…means *bright, gorgeous, magnificent, resplendent, shining,* or *sumptuous*. Here it refers to *clothing that is obviously expensive and belongs to someone with financial means*."[4]

Today we would describe this as someone who comes to church, flashing his or her jewelry and wearing designer-level clothes. This person is so decked out in the finest of fashions that people can't help but notice.

The Deeply Destitute and Outcast Also Attend Church

James contrasted the image of the wealthy individual who commanded attention by wearing extravagant clothes and shiny jewelry with someone at the opposite end of the social spectrum. The disparity is striking — one arrives adorned in luxury, while the other carries the visible weight of hardship.

The *Renner Interpretive Version* (*RIV*) of James 2:2 concludes by saying:

> **…And then there also comes into your congregation an impoverished person dressed in dirty, grimy, and offensively stinking clothes.**

For this final portion of James 2:2, we will look at several footnotes, the first being Footnote 237, which says, "The word 'then' is a translation of the word *de*, a conjunction intended to make a dramatic comparison."[5] That is what James was doing in this passage — he was dramatically contrasting the wealthy man who comes into church wearing flashy, expensive clothes and a gaudy ring with the impoverished man, who was clearly living on the other end of the financial spectrum.

Our second pertinent footnote in the *Renner Interpretive Version* (*RIV*) is Footnote 239, which says, "The words 'impoverished person' are an interpretation of the word *ptochos*, depicting *one who crouches or cowers like a beggar — probably out of embarrassment for the way he looks.* It depicts *abject poverty*, thus *one who is beggarly, deeply destitute, lacking in earthly resources, or poor* or *one who is a pauper....* This word describes a person so destitute that he is deprived of the barest essentials for living. In fact, this word *ptochos* would normally picture a homeless person or someone who has to scrounge to find enough food to eat — a person society would consider down and out, financially ruined, and poverty-stricken. In addition to experiencing material and financial lack, such people also suffered as social outcasts, which added to their misery."[6]

Another footnote that helps us grasp what James was saying in James 2:2 is Footnote 240, which says, "The words 'dirty, grimy, and offensively stinking clothes' are an interpretation of a form of *rhupara estheti....* The word *rhuparos* depicts *that which is filthy, dirty, grimy,* or *rank....* As a phrase, it portrays *filthy, dirty, grimy, rank clothes* or *one who dresses as if he lives in squalor* and carries the idea of a person dressed in dirty, grimy, and offensively stinking clothes."[7]

So James was painting a picture for his readers, reminding them that every now and then both a wealthy man wearing expensive, high-end clothing and an impoverished man dressed in rags and fighting just to make it in life will walk into the same church.

Guard Against Treating the Rich More Favorably Than the Poor

Building upon his teaching on the dangers of prejudice and favoritism, James proceeded to paint this picture of how these believers were treating two vastly different types of individuals. James went on to say:

> **And ye have respect to him that weareth the gay clothing, and say unto him, Sit thou here in a good place; and say to the poor, Stand thou there, or sit here under my footstool.**
> **— James 2:3**

To understand the full weight of what James was saying here, let's look at the *Renner Interpretive Version* (*RIV*) of James 2:3. When we factor in the original Greek meaning of the key words in this verse, it reads:

> **And if, in fact, you are so enamored by the sight of the one who is attired with pricey clothes that you shift your attention, focus, and gaze favorably on him and tell him, "You sit here in the best seat — in a place of honor and respect." But then you tell the beggarly person, who is considered a social outcast, "You stand over there, in a place that is out of the way, less visible, and less honorable" — or you say to him, "Find a seat under my footstool or in a place more fitting for those like you who are socially less desirable."**

We would be wise to heed the old adage which says, "Never judge a book by its cover" because sometimes those who appear to be the most destitute and the outcasts of society are actually the richest people in attendance.

That is what happened at an auction Rick and Denise observed in Moscow many years ago. A man came in and sat at the other end of the row on which Rick and Denise were sitting. He was poorly dressed and looked like a rank outcast. When Rick saw him, he thought, *What in the world is that man doing here? Everyone else is fabulously dressed, showing off their wealth, and he looks like a vagabond.*

Much to their surprise, Rick and Denise watched as the man who was dressed like a pauper spent more money than anyone else in the place! In fact, he paid a million dollars for a tiny, little painting! Just by looking at him, no one would think he had even a dime to his name. But quite the opposite was true.

Being Prejudiced Leads to Devilish Discrimination

After James painted the picture of what was happening in his readers' church services, he told them:

> **Are ye not then partial in yourselves, and are become judges of evil thoughts?**
>
> —James 2:4

When we factor in the original Greek meaning of the key words in this verse, the *Renner Interpretive Version* (*RIV*) of James 2:4 says:

> **By making such distinctions between people, don't you see that you've allowed yourselves to become critics and judges with evil thinking and conclusions that are spiritually dangerous to your spirit and mind? Separating people in your mind and treating them differently according to what you deem to be their social class and financial standing is wicked.**

This passage is packed with meaning. For example, an important note in the *Renner Interpretive Version* (*RIV*) regarding the word "distinctions" is Footnote 252, which says, "The word 'distinctions' is an interpretation of a form of *diakrino*, a compound of the preposition *dia* and the word *krino*. The word *dia* means *through* and depicts *something that is done very thoroughly*. The word *krino* pictures *a verdict or final sentence pronounced as the result of a court trial*. After all the evidence is presented and the judge examines all the facts, a final verdict is issued and a judge hands down a final sentence in a court of law.

"But the compound word James used here pictures one who has wrangled back and forth with the evidence he has seen with his eyes. After weighing all the evidence, he comes to a conclusion and passes a final judgment. Thus, James was addressing believers who have inwardly wrangled about how to deal with people of different classes and social statuses. But rather than treat them equally in the sight of God, they wrongfully made a distinction in their treatment of people based on their physical appearance, class, and financial status."[8]

James unequivocally declared that this prejudiced way of thinking is evil. This brings us to Footnote 255 in the *Renner Interpretive Version* (*RIV*), which says, "The words 'evil…spiritually dangerous to your spirit and mind…wicked' are interpreted from a form of *poneros*, a word that depicts *that which is malicious or malignant*. In the New Testament, the word *poneros* pictures whatever is *foul, hostile, vicious,* and *vile*. It includes not only that which is dangerous to the physical body, but also that which is dangerous to the spirit or mind. It is *an act or attitude that is wicked, unholy, and impure in the sight of God*.

"The word *poneros* is often used in the New Testament in connection with the activity of demon spirits, and it lets us know that wrongly judging people is devilish behavior and completely unacceptable among God's people. This exhorts each of us to keep in mind that when we are born again and enter God's family and kingdom, no one is to be judged by skin color, nationality, financial worth, or any other superficial factor. In fact, the apostle Paul wrote similarly to the Corinthian believers."[9]

The Gospel Is an Economic Gamechanger

Paul wrote in Second Corinthians 5:16 about the new mindset believers are to adopt: "Wherefore henceforth know we no man after the flesh...." And the reason we are not to know anyone after the flesh is found in the very next verse, which declares:

> **Therefore if any man be in Christ, he is a new creature: old things are passed away; behold, all things are become new.**
> **— 2 Corinthians 5:17**

Friend, instead of being prejudiced against an impoverished person, we ought to give him the best seat in the house! If anyone needs to hear the Good News, it's this person. Remember, Jesus said He came to preach the Gospel to the poor (*see* Luke 4:18). The Gospel is an economic gamechanger, so rather than push a poor person aside because of how he looks, we need to give that person a front-row seat.

We must realize that the Gospel is never prejudiced, and Jesus does not prioritize people according to color, class, or nationality. He simply sees the hearts of the people for whom He died — and our Heavenly Father sees people the same way. Again, First Samuel 16:7 says, "...For the Lord seeth not as man seeth; for man looketh on the outward appearance, but the Lord looketh on the heart."

If we're going to be like God, we need to learn not to judge people by their exterior and ask the Lord to help us see their heart. The Bible tells us that all people have sinned and fall short of the glory of God (*see* Romans 3:23), which means the Gospel is needed by everyone. No one is too good — *or too bad* — for the Gospel.

STUDY QUESTIONS

> **Study to shew thyself approved unto God, a workman that needeth not to be ashamed, rightly dividing the word of truth.**
> **— 2 Timothy 2:15**

1. Outward appearances can be very deceptive. That is why Jesus warned His followers — both then and now — not to judge others according to the flesh, like the scribes and Pharisees often did. Read Matthew 23:27 and 28. What did Jesus specifically say was so misleading about these religious leaders? For a "big picture" of why Jesus was so repulsed by the scribes and Pharisees, read Matthew 23:1-33.

2. Jesus said we are always going to have poor people around us (*see* John 12:8), so we need to learn how to treat them with respect and dignity.

   - What will happen if we *ignore the poor*? (*See* Deuteronomy 15:7-11; Proverbs 21:13; 22:16.)

   - Who are you giving to when you *give to the poor*? (*See* Proverbs 19:17.)

   - In what ways does God personally get involved with the poor? (*See* Proverbs 22:22,23.)

   - How will God reward you for remembering the poor? (*See* Psalm 41:1-3; Proverbs 11:24; 28:27; Matthew 19:21.)

PRACTICAL APPLICATION

> But be ye doers of the word, and not hearers only,
> deceiving your own selves.
> —James 1:22

1. Read Psalm 12:5; 35:10; and Isaiah 41:17. Have you ever been the one who was poor, lacking in resources, and in desperate need of help from others? Were you out of work, low on funds, with no answers in sight? How did God's people treat you? How did the Lord Himself take care of you and provide for your needs? What wisdom can you learn from your experience so that you can help others who are struggling?

2. When we treat the wealthy favorably and snub or ignore the poor, God calls it evil (*see* James 2:4). Have you ever been on the receiving end of such prejudiced behavior? If so, how did it make you feel?

NOTES

[1]Rick Renner. *Renner Interpretive Version — A Conceptual Interpretation of the Greek New Testament With Footnotes and Commentary (James and Jude)*. Shippensburg, PA: Harrison House Publishers, 2024. pg. 60.

[2] ibid. pg. 61

[3] ibid. pg. 61

[4] ibid. pg. 62

[5] ibid. pg. 62

[6] ibid. pg. 62

[7] ibid. pg. 62

[8] ibid. pg. 64

[9] ibid. pg. 65

LESSON 3

TOPIC

We Are All One in Jesus Christ

SCRIPTURES

1. **James 2:1** — My brethren, have not the faith of our Lord Jesus Christ, the Lord of glory, with respect of persons.

2. **Galatians 3:28** — There is neither Jew nor Greek, there is neither bond nor free, there is neither male nor female: for ye are all one in Christ Jesus.

3. **Colossians 3:11** — Where there is neither Greek nor Jew, circumcision nor uncircumcision, Barbarian, Scythian, bond nor free: but Christ is all, and in all.

GREEK WORDS

1. "Greek" — Ἕλλην (*Hellén*): This pictures anyone from the Greek speaking world, but in the New Testament it's usually translated as gentile; it pictures anyone who is a pagan

2. "bond" — δοῦλος (*doulos*): the most abject term for a slave; it pictures one born into slavery

3. "Barbarian" — βάρβαρος (*barbaros*): anyone that didn't speak Greek or Latin or one who spoke it poorly

SYNOPSIS

In our last lesson, we learned that judging people by their external appearance is something that grieves the heart of God. This is especially true when we show favoritism to those who appear to be wealthy, while simultaneously disrespecting those who look poor and destitute. God calls us to treat everyone equally with dignity and respect. With the help of the Holy Spirit, we can carry out this charge and push prejudice out of our lives.

The emphasis of this lesson:

In Christ Jesus, all believers are equal. All distinctions of ethnicity, class, gender, and race disappear, and against all odds and societal norms, a single, unified body now exists. We are all one in Christ Jesus, and Christ is all and is in all.

A Review of Our Anchor Verse

Throughout history, humanity has struggled with division and prejudice — barriers that create deep wounds and fractures in society. Yet from the very beginning, the Church was meant to be different. To help his First Century readers — and believers of all generations — recognize and root out the sin of prejudice from the Body of Christ, James wrote:

> **My brethren, have not the faith of our Lord Jesus Christ, the Lord of glory, with respect of persons.**
>
> **—James 2:1**

These words carried profound weight, challenging early believers to break free from the biases ingrained in their culture and embrace the radical love found in Christ. When we factor in the original Greek meaning of the key words in this verse, the *Renner Interpretive Version* (*RIV*) of James 2:1 brings out its full depth:

> **My dearest brothers and comrades, whom I cherish and treasure, you must not be a respecter of persons. That is, you must not have, hold, and possess the faith of our Lord Jesus Christ, the Lord of glory — and at the same time judge others or base your acceptance of them by what you see in their external appearance.**

This message is just as relevant today as it was back then. God, our Heavenly Father, is not a respecter of persons, and He shows no favoritism (*see* Acts 10:34,35). As His children, we are called to imitate Him in all things (*see* Ephesians 5:1), which means we, too, are not to discriminate against others but treat all people equally.

A Revolutionary Way of Thinking

The apostle Paul made a powerful statement on equality in Christ that was revolutionary in his day. It is so important for believers of all generations to grasp that it is repeated almost word for word in two New Testament books. Under the divine inspiration of the Holy Spirit, Paul wrote:

> **Where there is neither Greek nor Jew, circumcision nor uncircumcision, Barbarian, Scythian, bond nor free: but Christ is all, and in all.**
>
> **— Colossians 3:11**

Then in his letter to the believers in Galatia, Paul said:

> **There is neither Jew nor Greek, there is neither bond nor free, there is neither male nor female: for ye are all one in Christ Jesus.**
>
> **— Galatians 3:28**

Paul's declaration truly was unprecedented. In a world divided by ethnicity, class, gender, and race, he proclaimed that in the Body of Christ, there's no Jew or Greek, no slave or free, and no male or female — we are all one in Christ Jesus. This was a radical message for his time, and its truth remains just as powerful today.

To imagine these different categories of ethnicity, class, gender, and race sitting together side by side in Paul's day and age was unfathomable because these diverse classifications rarely mingled. In the same way oil and water do not mix, all those various ethnicities, classes, genders, and races rarely, if ever, mixed. In fact, just like oil and water, they repelled one another.

For the people of the First Century to imagine these various groups declassified and united into a single body in Christ was completely profound and transformative. To help you have a better understanding of the vast differences between these groups and the hostility that existed between them, let's take a closer look at each one.

Greek vs. Jew

In Galatians 3:28 and in Colossians 3:11, the first major class distinction Paul mentioned was *Jews* and *Greeks*. The word "Greek" in these verses is the Greek word *Hellén*, and it pictures *anyone from the Greek speaking world*. But in the New Testament, it's usually translated as *Gentile*, and it pictures *anyone who is a pagan*.

Most readers assume the word "Gentile" simply means *non-Jewish*, and although this is correct, it is even more than that, as it pictures *anyone who is pagan*.

It is impossible to exaggerate how vastly different the pagans were from the Jews. While the Jews grew up worshiping the One True God, pagans were notorious idol worshipers from lands filled with drunkenness, debauchery, and multiple forms of unbridled sexual immorality.

The pagan world loathed the Jews, regarding them as narrow-minded and bigoted. Unlike the pagans who prided themselves on their open-mindedness in believing in a sundry of gods, the Jews strictly adhered to their belief in the One True God. The pagans generally deemed Jews as a people with a disgusting language and a bloody religion. Although there were rare instances in which the Greek-speaking world valued Jews for their business skills, they largely held Jews in contempt. Thus, refusing to mingle the Jews with the pagans was not just a preference; the antagonism Greek-speaking pagans felt toward Jews was deeply rooted.

Looking at the situation from the Jews' perspective was just as radical. Because of the Greeks' pagan beliefs and lifestyles, Jews similarly found Greek-speaking pagans to be disgusting. They especially felt disdain toward Romans, who had forcibly occupied the Jews' territories. The repugnance Jews felt toward pagan Gentiles was so acute that they did all they could to keep distance between themselves and pagans, whom they judged to be sexually deviant, perverse idol worshipers with no moral law.

For these reasons and many more, Jews tended to look upon Gentiles as an unclean, foul, polluted people. In fact, a devout Jew would have found a pagan Gentile so reprehensible that he would not even permit someone in that category to cross the threshold of his house. If a Jew felt that a particular Gentile seemed better than others, even to a devout religious Jew, pagans nevertheless were viewed as impure, contaminated people to be avoided if at all possible.

Circumcision vs. Uncircumcision

The second contrast Paul added to his list in Colossians 3:11 was *circumcision* and *uncircumcision*. One might think this is simply another way of describing Jews and Gentiles, but the word "circumcision," as used in Colossians 3:11, could also depict *strict, religious Jews* (as compared to non-religious Jews). The non-religious Jews were largely considered to be shameful in the eyes of religious Jews because they often were uncircumcised.

So the word "uncircumcised" in Colossians 3:11 likely refers to those *non-religious Jews whom religious Jews regarded as shameful*. And in this verse, it seems Paul was depicting a religious war that existed inside a single religious group. Deeply religious Jews who faithfully followed the rules saw themselves as superior to those who did not.

Therefore, the deeply religious Jews had little tolerance for the non-religious Jews, and this created extreme hostility between the two that was so cold-blooded that these two groups seldom got along in a civil manner.

Bond vs. Free

The next classification that appears in both Colossians 3:11 and Galatians 3:28 is the comparison of *bond* and *free*. The word "bond" is a translation of the Greek word *doulos*, which was *the most abject term for a slave*, and it pictures *one born into slavery*.

The system of slavery was so entrenched in society that as far back as the classical period, Aristotle wrote that those born as slaves had inferior intellects and were biologically designed to be slaves. He even said that they should be contented to live in a subservient condition for the rest of their lives.

While this mindset is outrageous to us today, and it is disgusting to us to think that slavery was acceptable, Aristotle actually expressed that from the hour of their birth, some are marked out for subjugation, and others for rule.

Those born to rule were the "free" — a word that refers to *one born free and who possesses rights and privileges only belonging to the free*. The demarcation between bond and free was so stark that even if a slave was later granted freedom, he or she was still considered inferior to others.

Male vs. Female

When writing to the Galatians, Paul also added that, in Christ, there is "neither male nor female" (Galatians 3:28). The Greek text is so strong here that it emphatically means *male* and *female* distinctions simply do not exist in Christ in terms of partiality.

A mere suggestion by Paul that there was no distinction between male and female was one of the most revolutionary statements ever written in history up until that time. It makes it altogether strange when modern critics charge Paul of being anti-women. When in truth, Paul, inspired by the Holy Spirit, wrote the most liberating words that had ever been written about women.

In the First Century, there were societal restrictions that were applied to women, but not to men. For example, men could vote; women could not vote. Men could hold a political office; women could not hold any political office. This absence of women in key public positions explains why men are referred to by historical writers more often than women.

Men were allowed to receive a full education, while women were permitted only limited schooling, usually far less than what was available to men. Women's public lives were so restricted that they were not even permitted to shop in a public market. In fact, if a woman was seen in a public market, it was likely she was a prostitute because decent women were not allowed to shop there.

Men had many legal rights; women had few legal rights. Men freely attended public meetings and forums; women were usually prohibited from these meetings. In fact, the lack of women's experience in public meetings was why Paul found it necessary to instruct women in his epistles about what to do when something was said in a church service that needed explanation.

That is not the focus of what we're talking about in this lesson, but it's important to note, as many have not deeply studied the subject of men and women within the Church and have wrongly concluded that Paul was against women. On the contrary, he so liberated women that they were allowed for the first time to sit side by side with men in public meetings.

This level of equality was a culturally unthinkable development that was only possible in Christ. Prior to Christ, having women sit in a meeting with men would have never happened because the boundary lines between male and female in both the Jewish and Greek-speaking worlds generally did not permit it. But in Christ, those restrictive distinctions were — and are — obliterated.

Barbarian vs. Scythian

The last classification the apostle Paul addressed is *Barbarian* and *Scythian*, and it is only mentioned in Colossians 3:11. The word "Barbarian" is a translation of the Greek word *barbaros*, and it refers to *anyone who didn't speak Greek or Latin, or one who spoke it poorly*. According to the educated people of the time, those who didn't speak these languages or speak them well were regarded as lacking in culture, being uncivilized, and therefore were viewed as a lower class than others.

Paul also listed Scythians in this astonishing list of people groups, and Scythians were a nomadic people who originally lived in the steppes north and east of the Black Seas. Over time, they were divided into multiple groups of tribes, and they were viewed as "the barbarians of the Barbarians." While common Barbarians were deemed uncouth, Scythians were deemed the scum of the Barbarian world.

You could say the general feeling towards Scythians was something like this: "Well, we might be Barbarians, but at least we're not *Scythians*." So even Barbarians considered Scythians to be the lowest rung on the ladder in their world, and it would have been absurd to envision these various Barbarian groups sitting together peacefully in a social setting.

In Christ We Are One, and All Distinctions Disappear

So when Paul listed all these groups — which were each on the furthest ends of the spectrum and would have never naturally found commonality with each other — he made an astonishing claim: They were now all one in Christ Jesus. Against all odds and the societal norms of that age, a single, unified body had emerged, made up of these once-divided parts, with "Christ in all" (*see* Colossians 3:11).

As believers were baptized by one Spirit into the Body of Christ, they each became supernaturally and mysteriously blended, joined, fused, intermingled, and divinely melded into one single body of believers. Think of the magnificent supernatural unifying work God performed by His Spirit at the moment of the new birth. In an instant, classes and distinctions vanished inside this one new body, the Church.

When we put together all of what Paul was communicating in Galatians 3:28 and Colossians 3:11, we see that in Christ, all these ethnic, race, gender, and class distinctions just evaporate. Now we're all members of one Body, and in Christ there are no distinctions.

In Christ, all these distinctions have vanished. God does not see a Church of different colors or a Church of different nationalities. He sees that Christ is in all. That's who the Church is, and that's why in the Church, there is no room for any form of prejudice. We need to throw our arms open wide and embrace anyone who is washed in the Blood of Jesus and born by the Spirit of God. They are our brothers and sisters, and God expects them to embrace us in return.

In our next lesson, we will walk through several key verses in the New Testament and see how ethnic and class differences do not exist in Christ.

STUDY QUESTIONS

Study to shew thyself approved unto God, a workman that needeth not to be ashamed, rightly dividing the word of truth.
— 2 Timothy 2:15

1. All who put their faith in Christ Jesus are ONE in Him. The Holy Spirit makes this clear through Paul in Romans 12:4 and 5; First Corinthians 12:12-27; and Galatians 3:28. And Jesus prayed for us to experience this ONENESS in John 17:11 and 17:20-26. Carefully read through these passages and ask the Holy Spirit to give you a deeper, richer revelation of what it means to be one in Christ.

2. Prior to this lesson, had you heard it taught that Paul was "anti-women"? How does this teaching, which shines light on the First Century male and female dynamic, help you better understand passages like First Corinthians 14:33-35 and First Timothy 2:11-14?

3. Paul, inspired by the Holy Spirit, wrote the most liberating words that had ever been written about women when he penned Galatians 3:28. How does this verse and the concept of all believers being "one in Christ" help you see that Paul was actually one of the most pro-women voices of equality in his day?

PRACTICAL APPLICATION

**But be ye doers of the word, and not hearers only,
deceiving your own selves.
— James 1:22**

1. What new insights did you learn about the differences between Jews and Greeks; circumcised and uncircumcised Jews; bond and free; male and female; and Barbarians and Scythians?

2. Are there certain people groups with which you find it difficult to share the Gospel and include in the Body of Christ? If so, who? What is it about their nationality, economic or educational background, skin color, culture, or religious upbringing that makes it hard for you to accept them as a brother or sister in Christ? Be honest with the Lord and pour out your feelings to Him. Ask Him to surface any hidden fears or past hurts so that you can surrender them to Him and receive His forgiveness and His grace to live free from all prejudice, in Jesus' name.

LESSON 4

TOPIC

Ethnic and Class Differences Do Not Exist in Christ

SCRIPTURES

1. **James 2:1** — My brethren, have not the faith of our Lord Jesus Christ, the Lord of glory, with respect of persons.

2. **1 Samuel 16:7** — ...For the Lord seeth not as man seeth; for man looketh on the outward appearance, but the Lord looketh on the heart.

3. **Galatians 3:28** — There is neither Jew nor Greek, there is neither bond nor free, there is neither male nor female: for ye are all one in Christ Jesus.

4. **Colossians 3:11** — Where there is neither Greek nor Jew, circumcision nor uncircumcision, Barbarian, Scythian, bond nor free: but Christ is all, and in all.

5. **Ephesians 1:22,23** — And hath put all things under his feet, and gave him to be the head over all things to the church, Which is his body, the fulness of him that filleth all in all.

6. **Philippians 3:5** — Circumcised the eighth day, of the stock of Israel, of the tribe of Benjamin, an Hebrew of the Hebrews; as touching the law, a Pharisee.

7. **Acts 13:1** — Now there were in the church that was at Antioch certain prophets and teachers; as Barnabas, and Simeon that was called Niger, and Lucius of Cyrene, and Manaen, which had been brought up with Herod the tetrarch, and Saul.

GREEK WORDS

No Greek words were shown on the TV program.

SYNOPSIS

As we have seen, prejudice comes in all shapes and sizes and knows no boundaries. It affects all people of all nationalities on all continents, influencing young and old, rich and poor, male and female, non-Christian and Christian alike.

Often, prejudice is subtle and operates on a subconscious level. Nevertheless, it affects the way you think, speak, and act — especially in how you treat others. It may be that prejudiced thinking has caused barriers to be built between you and other people you really need in your life.

With the penetrating power of the Spirit of truth working in your life, those barriers can be bulldozed, enabling you to experience more freedom and joy in Christ than you have ever experienced before!

The emphasis of this lesson:

Ethnic and class distinctions disappear in Christ, and the church in Antioch proved it. It became the prototype for the Body of Christ, having leaders and members who were Jews and Greeks, slave and free, black and white, rich and poor, and educated and uneducated.

A Review of Our Foundational Verse

In addition to encouraging persecuted believers, James also equipped his readers with practical wisdom for everyday Christian living and exposed hypocritical practices in the Church. As we have seen, he opened the second chapter in his letter by saying:

> **My brethren, have not the faith of our Lord Jesus Christ, the Lord of glory, with respect of persons.**
>
> **—James 2:1**

When we factor in the original Greek meaning of the key words in this verse, the *Renner Interpretive Version* (*RIV*) of James 2:1 says:

> **My dearest brothers and comrades, whom I cherish and treasure, you must not be a respecter of persons. That is, you must not have, hold, and possess the faith of our Lord Jesus Christ, the Lord of glory — and at the same time judge others or base your acceptance of them by what you see in their external appearance.**

Here we see that having faith in Christ and judging others by their external appearance does not mix. First Samuel 16:7 says, "...For the Lord seeth not as man seeth; for man looketh on the outward appearance, but the Lord looketh on the heart." In the same way, we are not to pre-judge others by what we see on the surface. Instead, we are to lean into the Holy Spirit and receive His grace to understand people's hearts.

We Are All ONE in Christ!

In Lesson 3, we learned about how all believers are ONE in Christ Jesus. The apostle Paul talked about this throughout his epistles but really highlighted this truth in his letters to the Colossians and to the believers in Galatia. Under the divine inspiration of the Holy Spirit, Paul wrote:

> **Where there is neither Greek nor Jew, circumcision nor uncircumcision, Barbarian, Scythian, bond nor free: but Christ is all, and in all.**
>
> **— Colossians 3:11**

Then in his letter to the believers in Galatia, Paul said:

There is neither Jew nor Greek, there is neither bond nor free, there is neither male nor female: for ye are all one in Christ Jesus.

— Galatians 3:28

There are five important truths that are established in these verses about the Body of Christ. First, Paul said that in Christ, "There is neither **Jew nor Greek**..." (Galatians 3:28). This was a revolutionary statement because Greeks — which were *all non-Jews and pagans* — loathed Jews and regarded them as narrow-minded, bigoted, and disgusting. Likewise, Jews regarded Greeks as repugnant, perverse idol worshipers. Placing these two categories on the same level was revolutionary.

Second, Paul said that in Christ, "...there is neither...**circumcision nor uncircumcision**..." (Colossians 3:11). Rather than just describing Jews and Gentiles, the word "circumcision" in this verse depicts strict *religious Jews*, and the word "uncircumcision" describes *non-religious Jews* whom the strictly religious Jews considered to be shameful because they were often uncircumcised. Paul said that in Christ, this distinction was dissolved.

Third, Paul said that in Christ, "...there is neither **bond nor free**..." (Galatians 3:28). The word "bond" here describes *the most abject term for a slave,* and it pictures *one born into slavery.* And the word "free" refers to *one born free and who possesses rights and privileges only belonging to the free.* Although the world could in no way merge these two groups, in Christ, bond and free are seen as one.

Fourth, Paul said that in Christ, "...there is neither **male nor female**..." (Galatians 3:28). The Greek text is so strong here that it emphatically means male and female distinctions simply do not exist in Christ in terms of partiality. Prior to Christ, the boundary lines between males and females in both the Jewish and Greek-speaking worlds generally did not permit mingling. But in Christ, those restrictive distinctions were — and are — obliterated.

Fifth, Paul said that in Christ, "...There is neither... **Barbarian** [nor] **Scythian**..." (Colossians 3:11). The word "Barbarian" describes *anyone who didn't speak Greek or Latin, or one who spoke it poorly,* and Scythians were a nomadic type of people who, over time, were divided into multiple groups of tribes. They were viewed as "the Barbarians of the barbarians" and were the lowest rung on the cultural ladder.

Under the inspiration of the Holy Spirit, the apostle Paul declared that all these ethnic, race, gender, and class distinctions disappear. Now we're all members of one body, and "...Christ is all, and in all" (Colossians 3:11).

Paul's Pre-Christ Pedigree Was Impressive in the World's Eyes

It is important to note that Paul didn't just preach about the absence of distinctions and prejudice in the Body of Christ — he lived it. A careful study of Philippians 3 reveals what Paul thought and said about himself before coming to Christ. For example, in Philippians 3:5, he said:

> **Circumcised the eighth day, of the stock of Israel, of the tribe of Benjamin, an Hebrew of the Hebrews; as touching the law, a Pharisee.**

In this passage, Paul was describing who he was prior to becoming a Christian, and the items he listed amount to quite an impressive pedigree:

1. **"Circumcised the eighth day"** — This means Paul was among the strictest religious Jews.
2. **"Of the stock of Israel"** — This was the equivalent of Paul saying, "I am a pure-bred, pure-blooded Jew. There is no mixture in me." Clearly, there's a degree of pride in that statement.
3. **"Of the tribe of Benjamin"** — To understand this, you need to know the tribe of Benjamin was viewed as the best of all the tribes — the most cherished and prized of all the clans.
4. **"An Hebrew of the Hebrews"** — This was Paul's way of saying that everything about him was Hebrew — what he thought, how he spoke, what he ate, and how he lived. All the training he had received was Hebrew through and through.
5. **"As touching the law, a Pharisee"** — This phrase meant Paul was one of the most strictly religious, rule-following Jews around. Indeed, he said, "Concerning zeal, persecuting the church; touching the righteousness which is in the law, blameless" (Philippians 3:6). This was Paul's way of saying, "I kept the whole law," which seems an impossible task because there were so many laws.

Thus, before surrendering his life to Jesus, Paul was a Hebrew of Hebrews to the core who lived in a very exclusive world among Jews. He despised

Gentiles or pagans and had a growing murderous hatred for Christians. But all that changed when he encountered Christ on the road to Damascus.

God Was Doing a New Thing in Antioch!

After Paul got saved, he spent a short time preaching the Gospel in Damascus and then in Jerusalem, but when things turned chaotic and his life was in danger, the apostles put him on a ship and sent him to his hometown of Tarsus (*see* Acts 9:20-30). There he remained for about five years until Barnabas searched him out and brought him to a thriving new church in the town of Antioch, located in northern Syria (*see* Acts 11:25,26).

Acts 13:1 reveals to us the names of the leaders in Antioch:

> **Now there were in the church that was at Antioch certain prophets and teachers; as Barnabas, and Simeon that was called Niger, and Lucius of Cyrene, and Manaen, which had been brought up with Herod the tetrarch, and Saul.**

Five leaders are mentioned in this verse — Saul, Barnabas, Simeon, Lucius, and Manaen. Of these men of God, two had a Hebrew background, which were Saul and Barnabas. The other three — Simeon, Lucius, and Manaen — were Gentiles. This tells us clearly that the leadership team in Antioch was a mixture of Jews and Gentiles.

Naturally speaking, these people would have never sat together, much less worked together in ministry. Culturally, they were diametrically opposed to each other. Naturally speaking, there were great prejudices among the groups to which these men belonged. But God was up to something! He was breaking from past traditions, and for the first time, Jews and Gentiles were serving the Lord together as equal partners in the Body of Christ.

Where do you think Paul got the revelation that *in Christ* there's neither Jew nor Greek, circumcision nor uncircumcision, male nor female, bond nor free, and Barbarian nor Scythian, but we are all one in Christ? The revelation that all these distinctions disappear in Jesus came to Paul while he was serving in Antioch. It was there that he found himself serving side by side with people he formerly did not like and had a great deal of prejudice against.

Antioch Had Five Very Diverse Leaders

There is great significance in Acts 13:1, especially regarding not being prejudiced. When we take a closer look at the five leaders it mentions, we see that the church of Antioch could only have been brought together and held together by God.

First there was Barnabas. He was a Levite from the Gentile country of Cyprus, which was a region in Greece (*see* Acts 4:36). He was a distant Jew descended from the tribe of Levi, and because he grew up far from Jerusalem, it is likely he did not grow up around the strict religious community that was so characteristic of that city.

Second was Simeon. Acts 13:1 refers to him as "Simeon that was called Niger." "Niger" is the Latin word meaning *black*. So in addition to being a Gentile, according to scholars' speculations, Simeon was likely a black man from Africa and may have been the slave of a Roman family.

So serving side by side with Barnabas (a Jew), there was a Gentile named Simeon. In addition to the contrast in skin color, there was the contrast of a free man (Barnabas) working with a former slave (Simeon). This was extremely rare in the natural world.

Third was Lucius of Cyrene. The region of Cyrene was in Northern Africa. Hence, Lucius was a man of North African heritage. The name Lucius actually means *light* or *bright*, and it indicates that he was a black man who may have had a lighter color skin.

If you are keeping tabs on who is sitting in positions of leadership, you see that there were two black men on this team — both of whom were probably former slaves — along with a Jew (Barnabas).

Fourth was Manaen. Acts 13:1 documents that Manaen had been brought up with Herod the tetrarch and was, in fact, probably a relative of the family of Herod. This meant Manaen was a Roman and likely descended from the royal family. He had received a Roman education, and this was significant because educated Romans were raised to look down on foreigners as being uncouth Barbarians who were classified as "less" than Romans.

Manaen's position alongside other ethnicities and skin colors tells us he had broken free from the prejudices of his royal Roman upbringing. To work alongside two Africans who were former slaves and two Jews was not culturally acceptable in the First Century, and the odds of this happening were near impossible — but in Christ, this became possible.

Fifth was Paul. While serving in Antioch, he was still known as Saul. He had been born into a well-connected, tremendously wealthy Jewish family who were also Roman citizens. Being raised in a wealthy home afforded him the best education money could buy. He had also been theologically trained for his former positions as a rabbi and a Pharisee. Therefore, he was the most religiously instructed and possessed the greatest depth of scriptural knowledge of all his peers in leadership at Antioch.

Out of these five leaders, not one considered himself better than another. They were all equal partners in ministry in the city of Antioch. Again, that is where Paul got his revelation of believers being one in Christ. He learned that it didn't matter if you were Jew or Gentile, slave or free, royalty or common, Barbarian or Scythian. Christ is all and in all, and in Him, all distinctions evaporate.

Saul happened to be in the right place and in the right environment. God had placed him there purposely among people he formerly wouldn't have even spoken to, but his prejudice disappeared as he served side by side with them in Christ.

Mysteriously and Marvelously Melded Into One

Friend, we need to understand that in Christ, all distinctions and superficial labels disappear, and we're mysteriously and marvelously melded into one wonderful body. In Christ, there is no room for prejudice of any kind.

One day, when we all get to Heaven, no one is going to notice our ethnicity, our education or economic standing, our gender, our class, or the color of our skin. The only thing any of us will be focused on is finally experiencing the fullness of our redemption and worshiping the Lamb of God together. Praise God!

So why not start now? Let's eliminate all these distinctions and prejudicial attitudes and embrace who we are as the family of God. Let's humble ourselves in God's presence, and if He reveals that we have anything against any person or people group, let's repent and ask Him to forgive us, inviting His Holy Spirit to eradicate all prejudice from our souls.

In our final lesson, we will examine five things you can do if you have prejudice in your heart.

STUDY QUESTIONS

**Study to shew thyself approved unto God, a workman that
needeth not to be ashamed, rightly dividing the word of truth.**
— 2 Timothy 2:15

1. In Philippians 3:4-6, Paul listed numerous attributes and accomplishments he had before surrendering his life to Christ. But rather than boast or put his confidence in those things...

   • What did he do? (*See* Philippians 3:7,8.)

   • What became the driving motivation of his life?
     (*See* Philippians 3:8-11.)

   • What was he "pressing forward" to achieve?
     (*See* Philippians 3:12-14.)

   • What are *you* to do with these words he shared?
     (*See* Philippians 3:15-4:1.)

2. When Paul talked about us being ONE in Christ, he was describing the **new man** created in Christ Jesus. To help you understand what this new man looks like, carefully reflect on these two chapters in Ephesians. Then jot down what the Holy Spirit reveals to you about the new man.

   • **Ephesians 2** (especially verses 10-22): "God's Workmanship — One New Man"

   • **Ephesians 4** (especially verses 4-6; 15-25): "Put off the Old Man — Put on the New Man"

PRACTICAL APPLICATION

**But be ye doers of the word, and not hearers only,
deceiving your own selves.**
—James 1:22

1. The church in Antioch was quite a melting pot of people. As you take a few moments to reread the sections on the new thing God was doing in Antioch and the leaders He had handpicked to serve there, what new details are you discovering — especially about the five men mentioned in Acts 13:1?

2. How does the diversity of the leadership in Antioch, along with Paul's declarations in Galatians 3:28 and Colossians 3:11, help expand your view of the Church both then and now?

TOPIC

Five Things To Do if You Have Prejudice

SCRIPTURES

1. **James 2:1** — My brethren, have not the faith of our Lord Jesus Christ, the Lord of glory, with respect of persons.

2. **Revelation 5:9,10** — And they sung a new song, saying, Thou art worthy to take the book, and to open the seals thereof: for thou wast slain, and hast redeemed us to God by thy blood out of every kindred, and tongue, and people, and nation; And hast made us unto our God kings and priests: and we shall reign on the earth.

GREEK WORDS

No Greek words were shown on the TV program.

SYNOPSIS

What would your life be like if you ate the exact same food, three times a day, 365 days a year, for all your life? In a word, *bland*. Variety is the spice of life! And what can be said of food can similarly be said of people. When God created humanity, He fashioned a beautiful tapestry of all different kinds of people, each unique in his or her own way. Our differences add dimension and strength.

As you work through this final lesson, open your heart to the amazing work of the Holy Spirit. If He reveals an attitude of prejudice in you, agree with what He says and put into practice the five things you can do to effectively deal with prejudice.

The emphasis of this lesson:

Five things you can do if you have a prejudice are: (1) Become aware of your prejudices and ask the Holy Spirit to change your perspective; (2) once you acknowledge your prejudice, admit that you're wrong and repent; (3) spend less time with prejudiced people; (4) broaden your horizons and your experience; and (5) remember Jesus' blood is the same for everyone.

A Final Review of Our Anchor Verse

Actions speak louder than words, and when James heard that believers were discriminating against the poor, treating them less favorably than the rich, he called them to account for it in his letter. As a loving brother in Christ, James said:

> **My brethren, have not the faith of our Lord Jesus Christ, the Lord of glory, with respect of persons.**
>
> **—James 2:1**

When we factor in the original Greek meaning of the key words in this verse, the *Renner Interpretive Version (RIV)* of James 2:1 says:

> **My dearest brothers and comrades, whom I cherish and treasure, you must not be a respecter of persons. That is, you must not have, hold, and possess the faith of our Lord Jesus Christ, the Lord of glory — and at the same time judge others or base your acceptance of them by what you see in their external appearance.**

Aren't you grateful that God treats you in the same loving, patient, and merciful way He treats everyone else? The Bible says, "…God judges everyone by the same standard," and "…God is no respecter of persons" (Romans 2:11 *GNT*; Acts 10:34). Instead of pre-judging people by their outward appearance, He wants us to go below the surface and learn to discern their heart.

Five Things To Do If You Have Prejudice

One:
Become Aware of Your Prejudices and Ask the Holy Spirit To Change Your Perspective

In Lesson 1, we worked through a list of more than 40 different prejudices — some of them common and others uncommon. To help you become aware of what form(s) of prejudice you might be dealing with, here is a quick run through of that list:

- **Skin-color prejudice**: negative feelings against particular skin tones or those different from one's own.

- **Age prejudice**: the old are seen as useless, attention seekers; young are seen as inexperienced and selfish.

- **Class prejudice**: negative feelings against someone based on class, such as rich against poor; poor against rich; or poor against poor.

- **Married/Unmarried prejudice**: pre-judging people based on whether they're married or unmarried.

- **Educated/Uneducated prejudice**: pre-judging people based on whether they're educated/uneducated.

- **Debt prejudice**: negative feelings against those with debt.

- **Disabilities prejudice**: negative feelings against those with disabilities.

- **Physical-anomaly prejudice**: seeing people with deformities, abnormalities. etc., negatively.

- **Voice prejudice**: people getting turned off by someone's voice tone or sound.

- **Orphan prejudice**: a false belief that orphans are thieves and can't be trusted.

- **Homeless-person prejudice**: a belief that often deems all homeless people as drug addicts and alcoholics.

- **Gender prejudice**: males having negative feelings against all females, and vice-versa.

- **Women-bosses prejudice**: negative feelings against women being bosses.

- **Male prejudice** (misogyny): the false idea that all men are superior to women.

- **Hair-color prejudice**: negative stereotypes based on hair color. For example: the belief that all blonds are stupid or all redheads are hot tempered.

- **Birth-order prejudice**: false, preconceived ideas based on a child's birth position.

- **Bald prejudice**: negative feelings toward people who lack hair.

- **Tattoo prejudice**: a preconceived, negative bias about people with tattoos.

- **Bodybuilders prejudice**: a false assumption that bodybuilders are "all muscles and no brains."

- **Beard prejudice**: negative feelings against people with beards or certain kinds of beards.

- **Families-with-no-children prejudice**: a false assumption that couples without children are self-centered or self-absorbed.

- **Families-with-a-lot-of-children prejudice**: the false assumption that big families are made up of uneducated, stupid, and poor people.

- **Mother-in-law prejudice**: negative, stereotypical feelings toward a mother-in-law.

- **Name prejudice**: preconceived distrust based on a person's name.

- **Prisoner prejudice**: negative feelings against people who used to be prisoners.

- **Medication prejudice**: pre-judging people who take medication as being overly medicated.

- **Former-drug-addict prejudice**: the belief in the false notion, "once an addict, always an addict."

- **Weight prejudice**: pre-judging people because they're overweight or they're skinny.

- **Teeth prejudice**: negative feelings toward people with broken or crooked teeth.

- **Nationality prejudice**: a negative bias against people of certain races or mixed races.

- **Foreigner/Immigrant prejudice**: often manifests as a false idea that anyone who comes from another country is not living here legally or is taking away resources and opportunities from legal citizens.
- **City prejudice**: people in one city being prejudiced against people of another city.
- **Language prejudice**: negative feelings about people who speak a certain language.
- **Accent prejudice**: negative feelings toward people with certain accents.
- **North/South prejudice**: the false idea that Northerners are harsh and Southerners are slow or stupid.
- **Small-town-people prejudice**: negative feelings toward people from small towns.
- **Big-city-people prejudice**: negative feelings toward people from big cities.
- **Clothing prejudice**: pre-judging people based on the way they dress.
- **Musical prejudice**: people not liking others because they prefer a certain style of music.
- **Artistic prejudice**: people not liking others because they prefer a particular genre of art.
- **Political prejudice**: a preconceived view that everyone in a certain political party is bad.

Regarding political prejudice, we must realize that not everyone who identifies as a democrat, a republican, or an independent is automatically evil. Although they each have different views and preferences, it is wrong to lump everyone together and judge them as bad people. That is exactly what the enemy would want, so don't play into his hands.

Of course, the Church has issues of prejudice too. We see things like **worship-style prejudice; denominational prejudice; large-church and small-church prejudice; Bible-translation prejudice; pastors-of-small-churches prejudice;** and **pastors-of-large-churches prejudice.** Obviously, **religious prejudice** is a major issue causing many Muslims to hate Jews, Jews to hate Muslims, and on and on it goes.

Again, prejudice is not natural, and no one is born with it. It is picked up from an outside source, such as culture, society, family, friends, or the education system. Most often, it is transferred to a person because of the bad experiences of others or is developed from someone's own negative or traumatic experiences in life. Regardless of where someone gets it, all prejudice is ungodly, wicked, and has no place among the people of God. We must prayerfully discover what form of prejudice we may be unknowingly harboring and ask the Holy Spirit to help us break free.

Two:
Once You Acknowledge Your Prejudice, Acknowledge That You're Wrong and Repent

As you seek the Lord and He begins to reveal what is going on in your heart, you have a choice. You can reject what He is showing you and continue in prejudice, or you can agree with what He is saying, admit where you're wrong, and repent of it.

Repentance literally means *to change one's mind and go in a new direction.* In this case, it involves a decision of your will to no longer think about and look at people in a negative, judgmental way. Remember, God looks at people's hearts, not their outward appearance. If you ask Him, His Holy Spirit will help you develop this same perspective.

Three:
Spend Less Time With Prejudiced People

We tend to think and then act like the people with whom we spend time. The company we most often keep has the greatest influence on us. So be careful who you spend time with. Likewise, be aware of what you're watching and listening to on TV, radio, and social media. All these inputs affect you. Turn off the TV, radio, or Internet when you sense it is turning you against other people groups.

As you stay connected daily in relationship with Jesus and have your spiritual antennae up, the Holy Spirit will alert you to media that makes you think wrongly of a certain people group. He will also help you distance yourself from people who are a negative influence on you and help you find a new group of people who are more loving and Christ-like in their view of others.

Keep your mind free and clear so that you can think like God and not judge by outward appearances but by looking and discerning people's heart.

Four:
Broaden Your Horizons and Your Experiences

Satan uses the device of prejudice to keep each of us confined to our small space and our small thinking. When we bite the bait of prejudice, the enemy is able to steal some of life's most wonderful experiences from us. Our perception about certain people may be entirely wrong. So rather than just painting everyone in a particular group with the same broad brush, we need to broaden our horizons, expand our experiences, and make friends with someone in that group you tend to have a prejudice against.

Ask the Holy Spirit to help you begin reaching out to someone in the group that you're tempted to be prejudiced against. This could be someone of a different skin color or nationality, a foreigner who moved here from another country, or someone from a very different background than you.

Keep an open mind and heart as you speak with that person and ask the Holy Spirit to help you see what the world looks like through his or her eyes. There is something you can learn from someone else's lived experience. Even if you don't often feel the brunt of others' prejudice against you, try to imagine what life would be like if you regularly experienced discrimination like so many others do.

For example, in the world today, there is a widespread prejudice against Jewish people. For thousands of years, they have endured persecution, been ostracized by society, and been terribly mistreated. What would your life be like if you had to live under the weight of such discrimination?

This can be applied to any of the people groups who have prejudice leveled against them. Put yourself in their shoes. Prayerfully befriend someone in a group that you've been tempted to be prejudiced against and begin to see the world through that person's eyes. You may be surprised at what you learn and how different things look.

Five:
Remember the Blood of Jesus Is the Same for Every Person

As we noted in Lesson 4, someday soon, when we all get to Heaven, we're all going to worship and praise Jesus together. In that glorious day, no one is going to notice our ethnicity, our education or economic standing, our gender, our class, or the color of our skin. We'll all be in one group — the redeemed of the Lord who are washed in His Blood!

Revelation 5:9 and 10 says, "And they sung a new song, saying, Thou art worthy to take the book, and to open the seals thereof: for thou wast slain, and hast redeemed us to God by thy blood out of every kindred, and tongue, and people, and nation; and hast made us unto our God kings and priests: and we shall reign on the earth."

Friend, that's a picture of the wonderful Church of Jesus Christ! It is all of us — individuals from every kindred, every tongue, every nation. Therefore, if you have any kind of a prejudice in your life, it's time to deal with it because it's prohibiting you from growing and experiencing the fullness of Christ in the Church.

The only way to truly rid ourselves of *every hint* of prejudice is to fully surrender our mind and heart to the Holy Spirit. When we do, His grace will empower us to see people the way He sees them — as the precious creation He laid down His life to save. As the Body of Christ, we must resist the evil mindset of prejudice and do everything within our power to eradicate it from the Church. And now that we've seen how strongly God feels about this, it is our responsibility to invite the Holy Spirit to begin making changes within us.

If you are ready to take that step, here's how you can pray:

Father, I thank You that regardless of who I was when You found me, there is forgiveness and new life in Jesus! I'm washed in His blood, and in Him I am a new creature. Please help me get rid of every hint of prejudice in my heart and mind. I ask You to give me grace to no longer judge others by their outward appearance and instead see their hearts. I love and worship You, Father! In Jesus' name. Amen!

STUDY QUESTIONS

Study to shew thyself approved unto God, a workman that needeth not to be ashamed, rightly dividing the word of truth.
— 2 Timothy 2:15

1. If we are honest, *pride* is a major root of all prejudice, and the only cure for pride is *humility*. Carefully reflect on these vital truths concerning pride and humility. Ask the Holy Spirit to seal them deep within your heart and for His grace to put them into practice.

    - Pride is dangerous: Proverbs 11:2; 13:10; 16:18; 21:4

    - Humility brings blessings: Psalm 25:9; Proverbs 22:4; 29:23; James 4:6-10; 1 Peter 5:5

    - Humility thinks of and prefers others: Proverbs 25:6,7; Matthew 23:11,12; Romans 12:3

    - Jesus' example of humility: Philippians 2:1-11

2. The Bible provides some very specific direction regarding your friends and who you hang out with. Take some time to read these key passages.

    - Who you hang out with affects you (*see* Psalm 1:1-3; Proverbs 4:14-19; 13:20).

    - How "bad company" influences you (*see* Proverbs 22:24,25; 24:1,2; 1 Corinthians 15:33).

    - Steer clear of Christians living in sin (*see* 1 Corinthians 5:9-11; 2 Thessalonians 3:4).

    - Good friends sharpen us and help us (*see* Proverbs 17:17; 27:10,17).

    - Our strength and effectiveness are multiplied through good friends (*see* Ecclesiastes 4:8-12).

    What is the Holy Spirit showing you in these verses? Are there any specific adjustments you sense He's asking you to make to help extinguish the fire of prejudice and strengthen His influence in your life?

PRACTICAL APPLICATION

**But be ye doers of the word, and not hearers only,
deceiving your own selves.
—James 1:22**

1. In the program, Denise shared a story of how she was prejudiced against an athlete at her college, believing him to be insincere and just solely focused on sports. She was also frustrated because it seemed most of the money that came into her college went to fund sports programs, and not the music department she was in. But all that changed when this athlete shared his heart. In what ways can you identify with Denise's story? Briefly share any similar situation you've experienced and how the Holy Spirit changed your perspective.

2. Have you ever experienced prejudice or discrimination aimed at you? What would you say to the people who misjudged you if given the chance to share your story?

3. As you complete this study, it is most important for you to be honest with the Lord and invite Him to show you any form of prejudice that is affecting your view of others. Pray and, with the power of the Holy Spirit, begin to walk out these five steps to identifying and eradicating prejudice from your life:

   1. Become aware of your prejudices and ask the Holy Spirit to change your perspective.

   2. Once you acknowledge your prejudice, admit that you're wrong and repent.

   3. Spend less time with prejudiced people.

   4. Broaden your horizons and your experience.

   5. Remember Jesus' blood is the same for everyone.

A Prayer To Receive Salvation

If you've never received Jesus as your Savior and Lord, now is the time for you to experience the new life Jesus wants to give you! To receive God's gift of salvation that can be obtained through Jesus alone, pray this prayer from your heart:

> *Jesus, I repent of my sin and receive You as my Savior and Lord. Wash away my sin with Your precious blood and make me completely new. I thank You that my sin is removed, and Satan no longer has any right to lay claim on me. Through Your empowering grace, I faithfully promise that I will serve You as my Lord for the rest of my life.*

If you just prayed this prayer of salvation, you are born again! You are a brand-new creation in Christ! Would you please let us know of your decision by going to **renner.org/salvation**? We would love to connect with you and pray for you as you begin your new life in Christ.

Scriptures for further study: John 3:16; John 14:6; Acts 4:12; Ephesians 1:7; Hebrews 10:19,20; 1 Peter 1:18,19; Romans 10:9,10; Colossians 1:13; 2 Corinthians 5:17; Romans 6:4; 1 Peter 1:3

Notes

Notes

CLAIM YOUR FREE RESOURCE!

As a way of introducing you further to the teaching ministry of Rick Renner, we would like to send you FREE of charge his teaching, "How To Receive a Miraculous Touch From God" on CD or as an MP3 download.

In His earthly ministry, Jesus commonly healed *all* who were sick of *all* their diseases. In this profound message, learn about the manifold dimensions of Christ's wisdom, goodness, power, and love toward all humanity who came to Him in faith with their needs.

☑ **YES, I want to receive Rick Renner's monthly teaching letter!**

Simply scan the QR code to claim this resource or go to: **renner.org/claim-your-free-offer**

Connect

WITH US!

 renner.org

 facebook.com/rickrenner • facebook.com/rennerdenise

 youtube.com/rennerministries • youtube.com/deniserenner

 instagram.com/rickrenner • instagram.com/rennerministries_
 instagram.com/rennerdenise